# PRECAUTIONS

No mercy.

# PRECAUTIONS

## BY ROSHINAIE JOHNSON

"How long has that been sitting there?" a kid customer asks.

"I don't know," I say. I wish people knew how to put shit back when they decide they don't want it no more. Milk sitting with the chip bags. All this lifting and walking back and forth. I'm fucking tired.

I'm twenty five working at Pop's Liquor Store. It's not what I want to do, but it will have to do for now. I hope I'm not like my friend Nevayah who is twenty nine working here.

Pop's name is Mr. Harris. He's Nevayah's dad. I been working for him since I got out of high school. Even though Nevayah's older than me, we real close. We met in detention. When the teacher wasn't looking we wrote notes. I was in there for talking smart to my teacher because she kept calling on me to answer all the questions, and Nevayah was in there for cheating on a test and skipping school.

"Leilani, some of the can goods are mixed up on aisle three. Get them together," Mr. Harris says.

I'm throwing the milk away first.

Mr. Harris is mad as hell when he calls me and Nevayah in the back. People are eating in the store and not paying.

One time this boy walked in with his breath smelling like toothpaste. Before he left I walked up to him and he kept taking steps back when I got closer. I stopped and asked him a question. I couldn't smell his breath, but I could see all the brown stains on his teeth.

It's only me, Nevayah, two of her cousins, Jacey and Paula, and Mr. Harris that work here.

We need more workers but Mr. Harris likes to drive expensive cars and go to clubs.

"What are we going to do about these damn kids?" Mr. Harris asks. I already told him to hire a security guard but he doesn't want to spend money on one.

I think Jacey and Paula told people the security camera doesn't work because when it was working nobody was stealing.

I want to tell Mr. Harris about his nieces, but I'm not trying to find out if he gone get mad.

I don't say nothing too because Mr. Harris knows what them people doing when one checks out with a pack of gum, one is in the back hiding behind the aisle, and another one is talking to one of us.

"We can work in threes every day," Nevayah says. "Have someone stand at the back by the coolers. Then we have someone that can see what we can't from the damn front," Nevayah says. Mr. Harris looks at her like she better watch her mouth. "My bad Pops."

"Tell me who's working overtime because I'm not hiring nobody else," Mr. Harris says.

We don't look at him.

"That's what I thought," Mr. Harris says.

A woman's at the counter hitting the bell. It's not making any noise. The open sign is facing me so the closed sign can be seen on the outside. "Ma'am we're closed," I say.

"I need some water for my baby boy," the woman says.

The little boy has the cutest face so I wish he wasn't hers.

"Two dollars," I say. She takes the water bottle then hands me her card. "It's declined," I say.

"What you think I'm some broke bitch?" the woman asks.

"I'm just telling you what the screen says," I say.

She snatches her card, grabs her son's arm and leaves.

When we get home Nevayah pulls out the weed.

Me and Nevayah been living together for years so we can do what we want without money holding us back.

"Daysha and Yana on they way," I say to Nevayah. She on the toilet smoking.

I put chairs on the balcony.

"Aye, put some music on," Nevayah says.

I play some music.

While I make the drinks Daysha and Yana walk in. I met them through Nevayah at a party. Both of them are twenty seven.

"Where is Nevayah?" Daysha asks. "I know she here. I smelled the weed down the hall."

"In the bathroom," I say. "Help me with the drinks."

Me, Daysha and Yana go on the balcony and put our glasses together.

"Here's to another day celebrating us," Yana says.

We take our shots.

Nevayah comes out the bathroom. "How nice of ya'll to wait on me," she says.

"It was nice, because you sure as hell didn't wait on us to smoke," Yana says.

"Anyways, to life and God still given us breath in our bodies," Nevayah says and takes her shot.

Over all the years we've known each other, there's only been two fights.

One was when Nevayah smoked the rest of the blunt

when Yana stepped out to buy our food. Yana snapped.

The other fight was between me and Yana. She stayed the night and got loud with her coworker. We had just got done smoking and drinking, so I was knocked out. I took her phone, cussed out her coworker, then her.

Me and my girls fight, but we're still tight.

"Aye Leilani," Nevayah says. "Does your leg still hurt?"

The other day I was talking to this man when we were all at the mall. Everything was fine until I tripped over my feet.

"Daysha you not still mad about Kenny are you?" Nevayah asks.

"What happened?" I ask.

"He pushed her against the stove," Nevayah says. "I walked in and threw his ass on the floor. I wanted to throw the hot water on him but didn't want to take a chance on him needing the ambulance. Ya'll know I wasn't supposed to be there. I don't got time for Daysha's parents." None of us want to deal with the strict Vine's.

"You done with him now?" Yana asks.

Daysha says yes.

We dance.

Then me and the girls get close on the couch.

We're talking about this boy named Bennie that used to have a crush on Yana.

"He never introduced himself whatsoever," Yana says.

"Did you think he was cute?" I ask.

"He was alright," Yana says.

"How much money you make off them roses he gave you?" Nevayah asks.

"Nobody wanted that shit," Yana says.

I'm jogging around the neighborhood.

There's a gang on my block. One wanted to hook up with me and I said no. People talk too much and underestimate how much I can hear by sitting by the window.

I get cleaned up and go to my Grandma Cedes house to eat. And that's pronounced Say – Dees like the end of Mercedes.

"Can you tell me how you eat like this all the time, don't work out and still keep your figure?" I ask my grandma.

"What makes you think I don't work out?" Grandma Cedes asks then winks at me. She's hinting that she's putting work in the bedroom. "High metabolism," Grandma Cedes says.

"Wasup Aunt Lani?" my Uncle Cameron asks. I say hi. Cameron calls me 'aunt' because I'm older than him, but he's my uncle. My Aunt Genessa, Aunt Larissa, and Aunt Lisa are over thirty.

Cameron overdoes his plate. "You coming with us next week?" Cameron asks me. They're going to visit my dad in prison and want me to go. He killed my mother. I don't think so.

My mom was drinking heavy one night. She started pushing and slapping my dad. She screamed, "You need to bring home more money! The bills are behind! I'm sick of living like this!" My dad didn't fight back until my mom threw pictures with glass shields at his face. My mom got a knife and my dad grabbed her and threw her against the glass mirror.

I was four.

"Why do you visit him?" I ask.

"Because he's your father," Grandma Cedes says. "It was an accident. Stop acting like your mother was a saint."

"He messed up our family," I say. "You had four beautiful daughters…"

"And now I have three and a son," Grandma Cedes says. "Leana was the only unappreciative child I had. Materialistic, never happy with what she had. Always trying to make us miserable when she was. She's the apple that was spoiling my whole tree. You've seen her fight her sisters over stuff that people put in her head. Well past the age of thirty she still acted like a child."

"I raised all my kids the same," I mouth those words as my grandma says them.

I hear cars pulling up.

My aunts are here with my cousins, Riley, Mya, Terra, and Linda. Riley is my Aunt Genessa's, Mya and Terra are my Aunt Larissa's, and Linda is my Aunt Lisa's.

It's time to go.

"Leilani you know I loved my daughter," Grandma Cedes says. "Stay. You're the only child she had."

"Like you care," I say.

"Hi Leilani," my Aunt Genessa says. I say hi and pull the fuck off.

I hate hearing my cousins say mom.

"How you want it?" Yana asks.

I'm looking in the mirror. "I think I want it up," I say. Yana puts my hair in a ponytail. "No down," I say. Yana lets go of my hair. "Shit. I can't decide." Yana's combing it. "Up." Yana doesn't touch my hair again. "Hold on. If I wear it up then if I…" It's a little girl getting her hair done next to me.

"You and Dave getting together tonight?" Yana asks. I say yes. David is a good friend of mine.

"Girl save your money," Yana says.

"Hey ladies," Travis the DVD man says. "All I got are comedies today."

"I'm good," Yana says.

"Me too," I say.

"So what you want?" Yana asks. "If he hitting it right curls will fall."

"That's true," I say.

"That's if he can go for a long time," Yana says.

"Playing or not, can you talk lower?" I ask.

"Why?" Yana asks. "Everybody in here has satellite ears."

While Yana shampoos my hair I think about David. He's a personal assistant for celebrities. I met him at my friend Jessica's graduation party. That same day I thought about enrolling in college.

Nevayah put me on with her pops when I told her I wasn't going.

Yana curls my hair.

"You look beautiful," Yana says to me.

"I love it," I say. "Where you headed?" I ask when we get outside.

"Home," Yana says. "You want to come?"

We talk about David on the ride. "Make sure you strap up," Yana says to me.

"I know," I say. "I'm not trying to have no babies no time soon."

"I hear that," Yana says. "I like spending time with my girls, kid free."

Me and Yana drink and talk about this man named Joseph she was pursuing but stopped. "The cigarettes got his throat all fucked up," Yana says. "That's why I just do weed. Fuck all that."

After we talk about Joseph I go home.

Nevayah got called in to work so I'm alone getting ready for the all-white party tonight with David for the most popular DJ in L.A., Tony Live.

I hear Nevayah outside talking to David. She comes in with tickets to celebrity parties. "Your man outside," she says. I say thanks. "You coming back tonight?" she asks. I say no.

David opens my door.

On the ride, he has me look in his glove compartment for a key and I find a ring.

"Who's the lucky girl?" I ask.

"I'm looking at her," he says. "Think about it."

The parking lot is a party itself.

"Let me get two shots," David says to the bartender.

I roll a blunt. "I love to see that shit," David says.

We hit it and David passes it to the man next to him.

"You look good," the girl with David's new friend says.

I say thanks and introduce me and David.

"I'm Vikki," the girl says.

"I'm Aaron," her man says. "Tony over there acting a fool." DJ Tony is smoking, drinking, and talking to women.

"Baby you want another drink?" Aaron asks Vikki.

"If you want to talk longer just say it," Vikki says.

"Don't act stupid and get your ass fucked on this dance floor," Aaron says.

"Boy please," Vikki says.

"So where ya'll going after this?" I ask.

"Outside," Vikki says. "Girl where you from?"

"Georgia," I say.

"Yes babe, I knew it," Vikki says. "Me too." I lead the way to the dance floor.

I dip down and come back up with my ass rubbing against David.

We say bye to Aaron and Vikki.

I cuddle next to David in the cab. The driver watches us kiss every time we hit a red light.

David gives his friend that drove his car some money and pays for him to use the cab.

When we get in his house he undresses me, kisses me, cups my ass and bites the cheeks, then eats my pussy. He spells my last name on it: Y. O. U. N. G., then falls asleep.

.

Jacey and Paula are doing inventory and I'm at the register looking at pictures David sent me from the all-white party.

The two kleptomaniacs are coming up to me.

"Someone opened these," Jacey says holding batteries. "You want them?"

"You left a wrapper on the floor back there," I say.

"That's not mine," Jacey says.

"Oh excuse me," I say. "The wrapper your friend left back there."

"We don't know whose eating shit," Paula says.

"Can you pick it up?" I ask.

They walk away.

I go shopping with Daysha at the store she works at, Nice Fits.

I get clothes and jewelry from Charley and Char's brand called Charm.

"You like these?" Daysha asks holding up jeans. I say yes and she puts them in the basket.

I get clothes from Ariel and Aries brand called Arise. Daysha grabs Arise perfume.

I grab a Rich Rider dress. Daysha grabs workout sets. "I figured you could use a lot of these," she says.

"Damn, ya'll get me something?" Yana asks when me and Daysha walk in. Daysha says yes and Yana tries on a dress. "How this look on me?" Yana asks.

"Like you need to lose a pound," Nevayah says.

"You look good," I say.

"Damn!" Yana yells.

"Shit!" I yell.

"What the fuck!" Daysha yells.

Someone's honking.

"Hurry up and see who it is!" I yell.

Daysha looks out the window, "Who drives a white Rolls Royce?"

"Come with me downstairs Lani," Nevayah says.

"For real?" Daysha says.

"What?" Nevayah asks. "You want to come?"

"Girl, hell no," Daysha says.

The horn is still going.

"Can ya'll please go?" Yana asks.

Me and Nevayah get in the car with her weed man.

I'm gone be higher before we get back upstairs.

"Wasup Pierre?" Nevayah asks.

"Shit you know," Pierre says. "Just getting this money."

"This one of my best friends Leilani," Nevayah says.

I say hi to the young looking drug dealer who looks like he just got legal today and is fresh from the high school hallways.

"Can I call you Lani for short?" Pierre asks. I say yes.

"We all call her that," Nevayah says.

"For real?" Pierre asks. "That's cool. It's nice to meet more of your peoples," he says. "What ya'll was up there doing?"

"Shit," Nevayah says. "Waiting on your ass to get shit started."

16

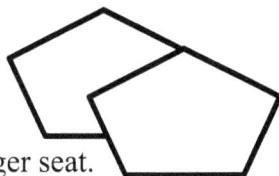

"I feel that," Pierre says.

He has two guns under the passenger seat.

"What you been up to?" Nevayah asks. Pierre smiles. "I know what that means."

"What?" Pierre asks. "It ain't got shit to do with no woman." He's scaling the weed. "Have you heard about Kareem?" Nevayah says no. "He found that nigga that popped his brother."

"Damn," Nevayah says.

"They found Kareem's ass the next day," Pierre says. "He fucked."

"Fuck," Nevayah says. "Roll one up for me."

"This one on me," Pierre says. "Moss Terrace. That's the nigga he killed. Moss killed Kahleel and Kareem killed his ass."

I'm not trying to hear about death all night. "Shit I want my drink now," I say.

Pierre takes out a liquor bottle. I take a shot out the bottle and Nevayah takes two. She pays him and we say bye. "He gets all his supplies from his brother," Nevayah says. "A cop. So if anything goes wrong we'll be out in less than an hour. You like his guns?"

"You knew that shit was under there?" I ask.

"Shit you heard what we talked about," Nevayah says. "We might need that shit."

"How you meet him?" I ask.

"Who Kareem?" Nevayah asks.

"No," I say. "Pierre."

"He's Neil's friend," Nevayah says. Neil is Nevayah's oldest brother.

Yana and Daysha are sitting on the counter drinking

when we walk in.

"How ya'll gone get fucked up without us?" Nevayah asks.

Yana grabs the blunt off the table. "Weed Wars gone have to be another night," she says. "I need it now."

"Why you need the weed so quick?" Daysha asks Yana.

"Look," Yana says. "Ya'll not gone be getting on my case all night." I give my girl a hug while she rolls the blunt and say, "I love you."

"Yana hurry up with the weed," Nevayah says. "Matter of fact, let me roll another one while you do that, that way we good."

"You know you can't reject no hug from me," I say and give Nevayah a hug.

"Since there's hugs and blunts, let me pour up some more," Daysha says.

Me, Daysha and Nevayah are staring at Yana smoke. When she remembers we're in the room Daysha asks, "You been abstinent for a while?"

Me and Nevayah turn our heads. "Ya'll can laugh," Yana says.

"Yana my mom coming to the shop tomorrow," Daysha says.

"All that laughing and now you want me to do your mom's hair?" Yana asks.

"Come on friend," Daysha says.

"Girl you know I got you," Yana says.

"Alright let's get it in," Daysha says.

Nevayah's putting the cards in stacks so we can play Kings Cup.

We start with two shots in our system. Whoever pulls a

king has to take another shot and pretend to have phone sex. If it's bad, then she has to drink the cup in the middle which has two shots in it.

"Damn Lani," Yana says. "How much longer?"

"It's been three seconds," I say.

"Exactly," Nevayah says. "That's too damn long in cards."

"Lani you done touched three piles," Yana says. "Come on."

"Girl take your time," Daysha says. She fucked up too. I pick up the pile closest to Nevayah.

"Hopefully Heaven being in your name will give me luck," I say.

"You know her name has never given us luck," Daysha says. "It needs another E."

"The weed ya'll smoking that got ya'll on one didn't come from our backyard," Nevayah says.

"Lani what card you get?" Nevayah asks.

"I see the weed and liquor got ya'll fucked up," I say.

"Girl stop playing," Daysha says.

I show them the Ace of Hearts.

"I'm done," I say.

"No you not," Nevayah says. "We still got cards left."

"I meant with my damn turn," I say.

The next round I pull a King and take another shot.

I'm trying to get to the fridge.

"I don't think so," Yana says. "No juice."

I put my sexy face on. "Lani what the fuck is that?" Yana asks.

"Massage me," I say in my sexy voice.

"Oh okay," Yana says. "I see you gone try to fix

19

whatever the hell you just did."

"Bring your hands forward and rub my chest," I say.

"Go ahead and drink the cup Lani," Nevayah says.

"Lani," Yana says.

"Shut up," I say and drink the cup in the middle.

Yana pulls the next king.

"I'm rubbing my ass wishing it was you," Yana says.

"Girl what you doing?" Daysha asks. Yana is on the table popping her ass.

I spend my off day lounging around the apartment.

David texts me to see what I'm up to. I tell him nothing. I'm too hungover.

"Get dressed," David says.

The nail shop isn't packed today.

I get my toes and nails painted red with black designs.

I hear a girl scream in the back.

"What's wrong with her?" I ask the worker.

"She get her," she touches her coochie area, "wax."

"Guess I'm used to it," I say.

When we get to David's place he gets on his knees and eats me.

I'm taking Cameron to basketball practice.

"Riley asked if you're coming to her 5th birthday party," he says.

"I'll think about it," I say.

"Why do you talk to me and not them?" Cameron asks.

"You're the only uncle I have," I say.

"Mom said to come by for dinner," Cameron says. "You can bring friends if you want."

"When are we going back to your grandma's?" Nevayah asks.

"I don't know," I say. "I haven't invited anyone to my grandma's since my mom died. I do what I need to so I don't break down in front of people."

"I miss your mom," Nevayah says. "I know how tough it is to deal with a death. It's not tough for you?" I say yes. "So why you shaking your head?"

"I'm looking in the kitchen trying to figure out what's burning," I say.

"Oh shit," Nevayah says. "Damn!"

"What?" I ask.

"The pizza rolls," she says. "Damn!"

They overcooked.

"Almost there," David says. We're hiking. "How you feel?" he asks.

"Like I deserve to eat breakfast, lunch, and dinner at my grandma's," I say.

"I like it out here," David says.

"Skyscrapers looking like regular buildings is a problem," I say. "I want to go back down."

I'm wiping his neck with my towel.

"What do you want to do in life Leilani?" David asks. I say I don't know.

"You do have dreams outside of the liquor store right?" David asks.

"No," I say. "I don't care for no more than I got. My mother was my everything. If she was here I would've went to college."

"You should go," David says.

"I don't want to," I say.

"Don't you think your mother would want you to?" he asks.

"Understand I do what I have to, to keep my head above water," I say.

I think about what David and Nevayah said when I get home. Because me, Nevayah and David are close, inviting everyone over for Sunday dinner at my grandma's won't hurt.

"Damn. How Yana beat us here?" Nevayah asks. We're pulling up to Grandma Cedes. "She can't be hungrier than me."

"Girl please," I say. "Even if you weren't hungry you would find room to eat my grandma's food."

"Hi," I say to my family. They all say hi back. Terra says hi to Nevayah and gives her a hug.

"Hi Aunt Lani," Riley says.

I pick her up.

"How come you didn't come to my party?" Riley asks.

"I was busy," I say.

"How you been Leilani?" my Aunt Lisa asks.

"Fine," I say. She's stirring the red beans and Terra and Linda are stirring the rice.

"Someone's at the door," Riley says stretching her legs down so I can let her go. "I'll get it."

"Riley go sit down," Aunt Genessa says.

Everyone in my family is in the kitchen so I know it's one of my people. "Yana, come with me," I say.

It's David.

"You're a handsome young man," Grandma Cedes says. "Come on in and let me introduce you to the rest of my family."

Everyone gets acquainted while we fix our plates.

The doorbell rings.

"I'll get it," I say. "It's Daysha."

Grandma Cedes says grace.

"Heavenly Father," Grandma Cedes says. "Thank you for bringing us here. We thank you for this food you have prepared for us. In Jesus name we pray, amen."

"Amen," we all say.

"Smells good Ms. Cedes," Nevayah says.

"Thanks Nevayah," Grandma Cedes says. "You haven't changed a bit since the last time I saw you."

"I know," Nevayah says.

"I know too," Grandma Cedes says. "When someone is sucking up to eat."

"You know I love you Grandma Cedes," Nevayah says.

"I do," Grandma Cedes says. "That's why I always joke with you like you my own. You can come by and get a plate whenever you want."

"For real?" Nevayah asks.

"Just make sure I'm home before you come," Grandma Cedes says.

"I like your shoes Ms. Cedes," Daysha says.

"Ya'll can stop now," Grandma Cedes says.

"You look really good Ms. Cedes," Yana says.

"Uh oh," Mya says. "Grandma got her hand on her hip."

"I just wanted to say it now so that way…" Yana says.

"That way I don't feel no type of way," Grandma Cedes says.

The kids are looking at Grandma Cedes.

"What?" Grandma Cedes asks.

"Feel no type of way," Terra says.

"I hear young folks say that all the time," Grandma Cedes says.

The kids tell everyone about school, grandma gives us tips on how to look thirty five when we're sixty, me, Yana,

Nevayah, and Daysha vent about our mom's putting perms in our heads, and David tells us about famous people he's met.

"Aunt Lani can I see your ring?" Mya asks. She calls me aunt but she's my cousin.

"You can see it from there," I say.

"She uses it to keep men away," Nevayah says.

"Seems like everybody wants to flirt these days," Yana says.

My girls always knew how to cover for me.

"You ladies look good," David says. "That's gone happen a lot."

Nevayah says one man said she was cute then tried to kiss her hand. "Anything to put they lips on somebody else but they wife," she says.

"They not slick brushing up against us," Yana says.

After we eat, we go outside and listen to music from Daysha's car.

"Girl turn it down some or play some old school," I say.

Daysha changes it.

"You better stop playing and put that rap back on," Grandma Cedes says.

My cousins can dance.

Aunt Larissa brings us some chips and dip.

"Look mom," Mya says and dances.

"I see you getting down," Aunt Larissa says.

Before I get in the car, Grandma Cedes says, "We all love and miss your mother."

"I know," I say. "I'm just having a hard time watc…"

"I know," Grandma Cedes says.

Me and Nevayah are bored as hell at work. We're looking through magazines.

The high school thieves arrive in the middle of the shift.

When they leave I get the camera. "What you doing?" Nevayah asks.

"Uploading this to my computer," I say.

"What?" Nevayah asks.

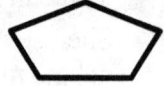

"Look at this," I say. "One buys something cheap while the other one eats."

"Let's make an example out them mutha fuckas," Nevayah says.

"You think I did this for my health?" I ask.

A lady gives her son a dollar for putting a bag of chips back.

Me and Nevayah are waiting outside this middle school that's around the corner from the police station.

Nevayah gets one of the kid's attention. "You want to make fifty dollars?" she asks.

"How?" he asks.

"Turn this in to the station for me," Nevayah says.

"What's on it?" he asks.

"What's your name?" Nevayah asks.

"Trevor."

"Trevor," Nevayah says. "I need you to say you left your camera at Pop's Liquor Store and play this for them."

"Fifty five," Trevor says.

"Excuse me sir," Trevor says. He sounds proper and not like the thug he was when he was talking to me and Nevayah.

"His parents have clearly told him how to make it as a black man," Nevayah says.

Trevor goes inside with the cop. "Let me know if you need another favor," he says when he comes out. "My names really Shawn."

"That boy is something else," I say when we pull off.

"You saw that shit too," Nevayah says. "He pulled his damn pants up before that damn cop saw him."

"You got to do what you got to do to live around here," I say.

The cops are at Pop's.

"Hi, I'm Officer Jensen and this is Officer McKinley. Are you the store owner?" Mr. Harris says yes. They go to the back with Mr. Harris. When they finish, Mr. Harris thanks them for coming.

"I told them to have a talk with the parents," Mr. Harris says. "If they do it again, I'll have them arrested."

"I'm putting they pictures on the poles," Nevayah says.

8

Daysha's parents are going on vacation and she's home alone.

Daysha opens the door with a drink. She tells us ours is on the counter. We sit at the bar.

"To the best weekend with my best friends," Yana says.

We cheers, cook and decorate the house so it looks like Las Vegas Boulevard.

"This the best we ever set this house up," Yana says. We're at the bar counter eating and drinking.

We dance.

"Oh shit," Daysha says when some New Orleans bounce music comes on. She's from the Ninth Ward in Louisiana.

I'm from Smyrna, Georgia. Nevayah and Yana from Los Angeles.

We go to Club X.

Nevayah leads the way to the dance floor.

Daysha tells Nevayah to look by the bar. A man raises his glass. "Pretend like you my girlfriend," Nevayah says to Daysha.

We walk into Las Vegas Boulevard back at the house. We're back to dancing, taking shots, smoking weed, and eating. Nevayah's dancing on the table to this fast ass bounce music.

"You stay rearranging your room," Yana says to

Daysha.

"Makes me feel like I just moved in," Daysha says.

Yana's looking at a picture of Daysha in middle school. Daysha puts it on her nightstand face down. "You were cute," Yana says.

We talk about all the hell we gave our teachers back in grade school. We had smart ass mouths when we didn't want to do something.

Nevayah's opening the window. "What you looking at?" Yana asks her.

"Nothing. I just want some air," Nevayah says. I stand next to her.

"Me too," I say. "I think we should go to an NBA game and get a baller."

"Yep," Yana says standing next to me. "Talent and money."

"And we'd be able to fly wherever we want," Daysha says coming next to us.

"I'm happy with what I got," Nevayah says. "Friends, a job, and my weed." She sparks the blunt.

"This would be a pretty picture," Yana says.

"I think God was listening," Daysha says. "Brandon put that camera up." The neighbors little boy has his phone pointed to us. "He's three," Daysha says. "He shouldn't know how to use it."

"He's cute," Yana says.

"Am I the only one that doesn't want to be on camera smoking weed?" I ask.

Brandon runs out of his bedroom. He runs back in with the camera light still on. Daysha closes the window.

Yana checks on the lasagna, I turn on the radio, and

Daysha and Nevayah get the wine.

We're on Daysha's bed looking at pictures. "I didn't gain any weight," I say.

"None of us did," Yana says.

"Do any of ya'll still talk to them?" Nevayah asks looking at a picture of us with our friends from high school.

We all say no.

"We threw down," Daysha says looking at a picture of us eating a late night breakfast.

"Sausage, omelets, hash browns, waffles, grits, butter biscuits, and bacon," Nevayah says.

"Damn!" me, Daysha and Nevayah yell. Yana's flash is bright as fuck.

"No more unannounced pictures," I say.

I put on my bikini and get in the Jacuzzi. Daysha's balcony leads outside.

"Here girl," Yana says giving me the blunt, a lighter, and a plate of lasagna. "I know you like to relax in the Jacuzzi so I'll be back in a few minutes."

I walk around the pool with my drink.

I choke on it because of the loud ass doorbell. Somebody won't stop fucking pressing it.

Shit. We usually don't have company on the first night.

Only Nevayah and Yana are in Daysha's room.

"What you got some party going on here!?" Kenny yells. "It's another man in here somewhere!?"

Me, Nevayah, and Yana hear a smack. We're running down the stairs and see Kenny on top of Daysha punching the hell out of her. He won't stop punching her. We're still running. Kenny punches Daysha harder and faster.

I'm kicking him in his ass, Yana's punching him in the

head, and he's still punching Daysha in the face.

"Get the fuck out of here bitch!" Yana yells. Kenny's drunk as fuck. He picks his leg up above Daysha's face and Nevayah hits him in his back with a metal baseball bat.

Kenny falls to the floor.

"Keep your fuckin' hands off her bitch!" Nevayah yells.

Me and Daysha are stomping on Kenny's face. "I'm so sick of you!" Daysha screams. "Son of a bitch! Fuck you!"

"This will teach his ass," I say.

Daysha gets the last hit with the bat.

"Leave his ass right here," Daysha says. "When he gets up, we'll let his ass out."

"When he walks out, he don't need to walk back in," Nevayah says.

"Thank God your wounds are small," I say.

"It's just a lot of blood that came out," Yana says.

We drink and sit in the living room. Nevayah grabs the bat. "Just incase Kenny decides to head any other direction than out that door," she says.

"Why you still fuckin' with him?" Yana asks.

"I love him," Daysha says.

"We deserve a better answer than that," I say. "Did he save your life?"

"I just want to know why you put up with him when you can get anybody," Nevayah says.

"If it's the sex, then I don't even want to hear it," I say.

"I wish he would get the hell up," Daysha says.

"Has it ever gotten this bad before?" Yana asks.

"No," Daysha says. "He drinks too much."

Nevayah sparks the blunt and says, "I want you to promise that when he walks out that door, his ass won't walk back in and you won't talk to him no more."

"She can start right now," I say. "It don't require no words for him to walk his ass out that door, and why the hell hasn't he got up yet? He's in the same damn position we left him in."

"But his damn blood keeps spreading on the floor," Daysha says.

I put my finger under Kenny's nose.

Nevayah checks for a pulse.

Kenny's dead.

9

"Where's my phone so I can call the ambulance," I say.

"Call the ambulance?" Nevayah asks. "We not calling nobody. He's not breathing."

"That's why we gone call some people so that he can," I say.

"I been to jail," Nevayah says. "Ain't no way in hell I'm going to prison."

"Since when did you not care about a life?" Yana asks.

"Since we were the ones that took it," Nevayah says.

"So what now?" I ask.

"The fuck do you think?" Nevayah asks. "We got to get the fuck up out of here."

"You think we're about to walk out this house and act like we didn't just kill somebody?" I ask.

"Where can we go?" Daysha asks Nevayah.

"So you want to leave him dead too?" I ask Daysha.

"It don't matter if it was an accident," Daysha says. "Four on one. We're doing time."

"So what are we going to do?" I ask. "Get a plane ticket out the country?"

"We're going to get rid of this problem," Nevayah says. "I had my mind made up I wasn't going to prison when I went to jail."

"He came over here drunk out his damn mind and beat my ass," Daysha says. "Ya'll defend me and he winds up dead. The worlds a better place and we're still in a bad position for getting shit like this off the streets."

"This is bullshit," Yana says.

"I'm not going to prison for even a damn day," Nevayah says. "So if you gone make that call Leilani, being that he's already dead, give me two or three days to get the fuck out of here. Don't call me ever."

"So it's like that?" I ask.

"It's like that," Nevayah says. "You want to give your life to the system, go alone. We need to scrape up all the cash we can, clear our registers at work and take every penny we see on the ground."

"And how long do you think that little bit of cash is gone last?" I ask.

"You right," Yana says. "What you got in mind? Besides going to prison. And for life at that."

"So I'm really the only one that wants to make an attempt to save his life?" I ask.

"Lani, he's dead," Nevayah says.

"Why don't we put his prints on a knife," Yana says.

"What part aren't ya'll hearing?" Nevayah asks.

"Did he drive here?" I ask Daysha.

"Let me see," Daysha says.

"Shit, did he just walk in the house?" I ask.

"He didn't," Daysha says.

"You didn't hear the doorbell?" Nevayah asks me.

"I'm not in the mood," I say. "How the hell you didn't see if the car was here if you opened the door?"

"It don't matter," Yana says. "What we gone do?"

"Call the ambulance," I say.

"Lani, this is real life," Nevayah says. "The cops going to look at things from every angle. One of the angles will lead to them asking if we put the knife in his hand, if we go

34

with that dumb ass plan."

"It don't matter what we do, he's dead," Daysha says. "Four women, one man. We going to prison."

"Do you even know any of his family?" I ask. "No right? You just been fuckin' him on and off. For all we know he is related to the damn deputy. You don't want to leave his body here. Dig up the tiles in the kitchen and we'll give him an inside funeral."

"Happy you came around," Nevayah says.

"You got no idea why I'm going through with this," I say.

"Yea," Nevayah says. "I do. Somebody scrolled across your mind. You don't want to let her down."

"Tell your Grandma Cedes hi," Daysha says.

"Whenever we get where we're going," Nevayah says.

"Ya'll think he told someone he was coming?" Yana asks.

"It's too late to be worried about being taken into custody," I say.

"Let's get rid of his body," Nevayah says. "Then we'll talk about the money and where the hell we're going. Wrap his ass up in something."

Daysha gets trash bags and towels.

Nevayah makes a phone call and says, "My cousin gone let me know when we can come through. We getting rid of Kenny's ass tonight. We need to come up with a plan tonight. My friend Trinity works at the bank. She gone be down with us."

"Why are we covering this shit up and still need money to leave?" Yana asks.

"Precautions," I say. "That's the main reason. Right

Nevayah?"

"Right," Nevayah says.

Cameron texts:

**Cameron:** Your dad died in prison.

**Cameron:** He got stabbed to death.

I'm not telling the girls my dad died unless they try to back out.

"I can get everything we need," Nevayah says.

"What about a disguise?" Yana asks.

"Look at this as a silent robbery," Nevayah says.

"What makes you think Amy will believe her life is in danger?" I ask. Amy is the teller Nevayah's going to.

"I'll give her a reason to believe," Nevayah says. "I'll set an example up across the street."

"What example are you setting up across the street?" Daysha asks.

"I'm not wasting time telling you no shit I'm doing by my damn self," Nevayah says.

A phone rings.

"It's not mine," Yana says.

"Me either," Nevayah says.

"It's not mine," Daysha says.

"It's not mine either," I say.

"Oh shit," Nevayah says.

She takes Kenny's phone and wallet.

We use all our damn strength to get Kenny in the trunk.

I ride with Nevayah to a man named JJ's garage. It's loud as hell in here because people are fixing cars.

JJ tosses Nevayah some keys and points her to a black car that's beat the fuck up.

"Aye KP," JJ says.

"Wasup Kareem?" Nevayah asks.

"Shit," Kareem says. "You know how it go. Give a couple people they don't like hell and they let you go."

Kareem and this man named D put Kenny on the backseat of the black car and follow me and Nevayah.

I'm riding in the back with Kenny and directing Nevayah to the bridge.

Kareem and D speed ahead of us when we get to it and park.

Nevayah speeds and curves, then we jump out.

I hear the car hit the water.

We get in the back of Kareem's car. He puts on the hazard lights and gets out. He's taking his gun out. A teenage boy is putting his headset on and powerwalking the other way.

Kareem shoots the boy and runs back to the car.

"Ya'll wouldn't of made it to tomorrow if I'd have let his ass live," Kareem says.

"I been around a lot of mutha fuckas like that," D says. "They walk off like they gone mind they business, then niggas end up in jail the next day."

"That nigga had a phone in his hand," Kareem says. "He was gone try and be the next internet star. Look at this shit." Kareem shows us the car sinking. "Ya'll wouldn't have been the only ones going to prison."

"You want to tell them about the kid?" Nevayah asks.

"Hell no," I say. "We got shit to focus on."

Daysha and Yana are drinking and smoking when we get back. Me and Nevayah do the same.

"What happened?" Yana asks.

"He's gone," Nevayah says.

"He shouldn't float for a while," I say.

Nevayah is nowhere to be found.

"She said she'd be right back," Yana says.

"Where you going?" I ask.

"To get some shit from my house real quick," Yana says.

"What you mad about?" I ask.

"I wish this would've never happened," Yana says.

"We all do," I say. "But at least we killed him, instead of finding out if he was gone kill her."

"Here," Yana says handing me Daysha's keys. "Go get you and Nevayah's stuff."

A body will be floating in a river soon. I'm ready to get the fuck out of here.

"Hey Leilani," this boy Dexter that lives across the hall from me says while I'm unlocking my door.

"Hey Dexter," I say and shut the door behind me.

I need to pack. A box falls out the closet with a funeral invitation.

Two of Nevayah's brothers, Nick and Nehemiah, are on the front.

There's a Los Angeles newspaper on the floor from the same box.

It says they died in a head on collision on their way to visit relatives. Her and her youngest brother Nathan rode with their dad.

Nevayah never told me her brother's died, and I'm not mad. She doesn't know my dad died.

Yana beats me back to Daysha's.

They're sitting in her room.

"We bleached the hell out of the floor," Daysha says.

"I smelled that shit outside," I say.

"We went over where Kenny was a million times," Yana says.

"I'm sorry ya'll," Daysha says.

I spark the blunt.

"That's not gone help us," I say.

"We wasn't gone sit there and just let him beat you," Yana says.

"We got to take care of business tomorrow," I say.

"We get this money and get the fuck out of here," Yana says.

We watch the news.

The reporter is talking about Mrs. Miranda Miles:

"Today a mother took her life after being sentenced to life for killing her husband, who killed her son and daughter. Police reports say that Mrs. Miranda Miles was filing for divorce from her cheating husband, Mr. Lonnie Miles, and was going to move once it went through. The divorce didn't sit right with Mr. Miles so he took the two people she cared about the most. When Mrs. Miles arrived home from work and saw her children dead, she decided not to call the authorities. She decided to track her husband down. She found him at his cousin's house and shot him with an unregistered gun. Mrs. Miles was only in prison for three days before she decided to take her life."

Nevayah's here. "All it takes is one push," she says holding a bomb then gives me a gun.

I get in the car with Daysha and Nevayah gets in the car with Yana.

Daysha pulls up to the corner across the street from the bank and Yana and Nevayah park in the back.

I got the gun in my purse.

"Be careful," Daysha says when I open the door.

There's a cop to my right and one by the entrance. If Nevayah taps her left hand twice on the counter I'm shooting the cop to my right, she gone shoot the one on the left and we both gone hold a hostage. Trinity's ass gets the money and we continue with the original plan from there.

Nevayah's walking to the counter. She's telling Amy when she cues her to go to the bathroom, take the bag, fill it with cash, take it out the back and give it to Yana.

One wrong move and she's dead.

Amy's looking at me now. Nevayah's telling her the baby bump is fake.

"Hurry up mom," a little boy walks in and says to Amy holding a congratulations balloon. Her husband, son and daughter are here to surprise her for her promotion that Trinity lied about.

"Wait for me at the car," Amy says.

Amy looks outside. Nevayah hits the remote.

The trash across the street explodes.

Amy takes Nevayah's wallet and goes to the back.

There's water shooting everywhere and people being carried away on stretchers outside.

I'm looking for Nevayah and Yana. "There they go," Daysha says.

We follow behind them.

I see Yana stuffing the money in the suitcases with our clothes.

We're headed to the airport. "Soon as we get settled in we're going to a bar," Daysha says.

"Fuck!" I scream.

"What the hell was that?" Daysha says.

"It sounded like another damn bomb," I say and turn the radio on:

*"Another explosion. This time inside the bank on third. The entire place is in flames."*

Daysha speeds and gets in front of Nevayah and Yana. She waves for them to follow us.

We pull over in an alley. Me and Daysha walk straight to Nevayah.

"What the fuck Nevayah?" I yell.

"Quiet," Nevayah says. "You think that lady wouldn't have talked?"

"You fucked up," I say.

"We don't have time for this," Yana says. "Let's get to the airport."

"After all this?" I ask. "I'm not taken no chances at the fuckin' airport."

"Come on," Nevayah says. "Four black women with connections to people that can make bombs?"

"We need to go," Daysha says.

"Ya'll the ones stopping like we not criminals," Nevayah says.

"We get to Mexico and make some friends," I say when I get in the car. "We learn our way and we get the fuck away from her."

"Why she do this?" Daysha asks.

"Because we already killed Kenny," I say. "Life is life." Nevayah done lost her mind.

"You think she would…" Daysha says.

"She not killing my ass," I say.

"You think she got more bombs with her?" Daysha asks.

"Don't matter," I say. "She can get them. The cops not the first people we need to be worried about no more."

"We need to see where her head is," Daysha says.

The next time we stop for gas we all use the bathroom.

I call Yana as soon as I get in the car. "We need to get the fuck away from her," Yana says.

"We all on the same page," I say.

Daysha gets in the car.

"Yana wants to get away from her too," I say. "What hotel are we going to?"

Daysha picks up her phone.

"Who you calling?" I ask.

"Nevayah so we can know," Daysha says.

"You call her asking questions and you letting her know we have suspicions," I say.

We get back on the road.

Nevayah runs over glass. The front tires of the car are

flat.

Nevayah didn't see this brown beer bottle glass that's broken in big pieces on this empty ass road.

She's taking the license plates off.

Yana's putting their bags in Daysha's car.

12

We're at a hotel in Mexico.

There's two little girls on the elevator when we get on. "Hi," one says to me when the door closes.

"Hi," I say.

"What's your name?" she asks.

"Leilani."

"Leilani what?" she asks.

"Leilani Young," I say.

"That's a pretty name," she says.

"What's yours?" I ask.

"Truth Ronald."

"That's a pretty name too," I say.

"Her names not Truth, it's Elle and mine is Megan," the other girl says.

"We're going to the carnival tomorrow," Megan says.

"And the next day we're going to the fair," Elle says.

The elevator door opens.

"It was nice meeting you Elle and Megan," I say.

"You too Leilani Young," Elle says. "I hope I see you and them again."

"I didn't know they had fairs, carnivals and shit like that out here," Nevayah says.

"Me either," Yana says. "Does the damn circus come here too?"

Nevayah puts her stuff down then leaves right back out the room.

"I saw another hotel down the street," I say.

"Let's…" Yana says.

Nevayah comes back in and puts a set of keys on the table. "One car not gone cut it for all of us," she says.

Yana turns on the news.

A list of everyone that was injured or killed at the bank on third is on it.

"Man turn this shit off," Nevayah says. "Let's focus on us and what we gone do."

I take a shot.

Yana turns the news up.

"And there goes our cars," Nevayah says. "But they not saying shit about us."

Nevayah steps in the hall and comes back with phones. "Take whichever one ya'll want," she says.

"Do you care?" I ask.

"Yes I care," Nevayah says. "About everyone that died."

"How come you didn't tell us you were gone blow the damn bank up Nevayah?" Yana asks.

"Because she knew we wouldn't be for that shit," I say.

"I did this for us," Nevayah says. "We needed to get out of there. And not with our hands behind our back. After all the shit that's happened, I know ya'll not trying to fuck with the courts now." Nevayah pours another shot. "We not the only ones that gave up on the system."

"No one else dies," I say.

"No one else is gone have to die," Nevayah says.

46

13

Nevayah's rolling a blunt. "My boy grows this shit," Nevayah says. "Remember JJ?" I say yes. "He put me on to his people out here," she says.

We go to the store with caps and sunglasses. Yana's talking to Nevayah about the weed spots and me and Daysha are trailing behind them. "Ya'll come up with anything?" I ask.

"The next time she leaves, we get our shit and go," Daysha says.

"Ya'll want to play cards?" Nevayah asks when we get back to the hotel.

"No. My damn stomach acting up," I say.

"I just want to get high," Daysha says.

"How many days is all this shit gone fuck with ya'll?" Nevayah asks. "The people whose family's lives we ruined. We can't do shit about it."

"Fuck it," Yana says. "I'll play. Just stop saying that shit."

"Wake me up if anything happens," I tell Daysha.

I take a nap and Daysha's phone wakes me up. "It's my mom," she says.

"How she get the number?" Nevayah asks.

"I called her while we were out," Daysha says.

"Why the fuck is she calling you this late?" Nevayah asks.

"Calm down," Yana says. "What's wrong with you?"

Daysha's phone stops ringing then rings again.

"Answer the phone," I say.

Daysha puts the phone on speaker.

"Daysha where are you?" Mrs. Vine asks. "We need you to come help straighten up this house and we need you to go through your clothes and give us what you don't want so we can donate it."

"I'll do it when I get back," Daysha says.

"Daysha where are you?" Mrs. Vine asks.

"All of a sudden you care where I'm at?" Daysha asks.

"Give me the phone," Mr. Vine says. "Daysha bring your ass here tomorrow and get your shit out this house." He hangs up in her face.

"They know," Daysha says.

Mr. Harris is calling Nevayah from the store. "He would never call me from that shit when it's closed," Nevayah says.

I get on the internet.

Kenny's body is taken out the river.

Anna the news reporter says:

"Kenny Dane was found dead. Officials say he was beat to death before being driven in the river. Divers are in the river hoping to find something that will lead them to the perpetrators."

The camera shifts to a lady screaming and a man crying. "That's his parents," Daysha says.

"Your mom ever call you this late before?" Nevayah asks Daysha.

"No," Daysha says.

I type our names in the computer and nothing comes up.

"Nobody was on the bridge with us that night, except

my peoples and the kid with the camera," Nevayah says.

"What?" Yana asks.

"Nevayah's friends killed a kid that recorded us driving Kenny's body off the bridge," I say.

"It ain't shit for these crooked mutha fuckas to set us up," Nevayah says. "Going down for Kenny, robbery, the murder of that boy, bombing the bank. They will escort our asses straight to the damn chair from the gate."

"The only reason everybody calling is to get us back in the U.S. so we can go to prison," Daysha says.

"My pops wouldn't sell me out," Nevayah says and calls him back.

"Nicole where are you?" Mr. Harris asks. "I want to help you get out of this shit."

Nevayah hangs up. "He only calls me Nicole when the cops got me fucked up," she says. "We need to get some shit straight and get the fuck on."

I get a text:

Unknown: Send me an address. 7062. Three hours and there. Get rid of the phone.

February 6th, 2007 is Cameron's birthday. It's my Grandma. She always told me to keep our shit between us, and being that she's talking in code, "It's the wrong time for wrong fuckin' numbers," I say to the girls.

"Can I speak to the manager?" I ask the cashier.

"That would be me," the cashier says.

I make him an offer to have my grandma's message sent

to his store.

"Not a problem," he says.

When I get back to the hotel Yana says we're leaving tomorrow.

"I got someone bringing us fake I.D.'s and passports," Nevayah says.

"Where we going?" I ask.

"Wherever has four seats when we get to the airport," Nevayah says.

We're at another hotel. "Shit," I say. "Fuck. Roll me another blunt Yana please."

"I got you," Yana says. "Wasup?"

"My stomach acting up again," I say. "I think I just need to sit outside for a while."

"It's a basketball court around the corner," Yana says. "A little entertainment ain't bad."

I need a pay phone to call a cab to get to the damn store.

One of the games ended on the basketball court and one of the players is coming towards me. "Excuse me Ms.," he says. "Please give me a second to talk to you."

"Walk with me," I say. "You know where I can find a pay phone?" He hands me his. "What's your name?"

"Diego," he says.

"My names Terencia," I say. I call a cab and thank him.

"Anytime," Diego says. "I know we just met, but if you need anything, I'd love to help you out."

"That's not what you came over here for," I say.

"I was honestly going to ask to see you again," Diego says.

"If you can get something for me, we can go wherever

you want," I say.

"I'll do that," he says. "And give you a ride where you need to go."

He goes in the store and comes out with a box.

"Is there somewhere I can get away from all these people?" I ask Diego.

On the ride to his place, Diego says. "The manager didn't want to give me the box because the name on it wasn't Terencia. You're lucky the lady that dropped it off was there."

14

Aunt Genessa.

Diego gives us privacy in his garage.

"You're in deep," Aunt Genessa says.

"Why are you only saying me?" I ask.

"Fuck the other girls," she says. "You are my niece. Trinity turned herself in when Kenny's body came up."

"Everyone knows," I say.

"Just the police and everyone they're using to find you guys," Aunt Genessa says.

"Shit," I say.

"I know what's going on because I have a friend that works at the jail Trinity's at," Aunt Genessa says. "Nevayah told Trinity about Kenny. She regretted it and tried to kill her with everyone else in the bank."

"What are you talking about?" I ask.

"She stepped out right before the bank caught on fire," Aunt Genessa says. "Nevayah left her own connect for dead. All those wigs did was postpone ya'll being found. Daysha drove you, but none of the cameras can pick her out. Trinity's mouth did. All four of ya'll are nowhere to be found. No one has an address to find ya'll. They're going to believe every word that Trinity says. Trinity trying to get time off what she gets. All she was supposed to do was get Amy's family to the bank and a bag in the bathroom. She didn't know about the bombs."

"Nevayah didn't plant all that shit in there without help," I say.

"Doesn't matter," Aunt Genessa says. "Trinity's the one cooperating. You guys are the ones running. Nothing you say will be credible. If you're caught you're dead."

Aunt Genessa gives me a phone. "You guys killed Kenny, got rid of him, robbed a bank, and got out the U.S. before his body turned up. They want you to wander the streets. That's why your names not on the news."

There's empty envelopes in the box.

Aunt Genessa gives me a passport to Sydney, Australia, a wig, cash, a license, some other stuff, and says I'm staying with my grandma's brother.

"I need to get my shit from the hotel," I say.

"Forget your friends," Aunt Genessa says.

I go use the bathroom.

"What can I do for you officers?" I hear Diego ask.

I go to a window.

"Diego Martinez right?" the fat cop asks.

"That's right," Diego says.

"I wanted to know if you seen this girl," the fat cop says.

"No I haven't seen her," Diego says.

"What about you?" the skinny cop asks.

"No," Aunt Genessa says.

"If you do give me a call," the skinny cop says.

Diego comes to get me.

"They must've followed me over here," Aunt Genessa says.

"They want her to lead them to the other three," Diego says.

15

I tell Diego one of the girls will give me a ride back to his house when I get to the hotel. I go to the corner store for some water. I see a little boy crouched down in the aisle through the window.

Nevayah's robbing the place.

The little boy mouths help.

I can't do that.

I go back to the hotel.

"Tacara Sons is your new name," Daysha says giving me the passport Nevayah got me. "When Nevayah gets back we're leaving."

"I just saw her robbing a store," I say. "Nevayah Nicole Harris no more. Let's get the fuck out of here before we're wanted here too."

"When we get to the airport we're changing the flights," Yana says.

Nevayah's back.

"I'll be back," Daysha says.

I put my suitcase in the hallway and sit on it. Yana and Nevayah come see what I'm doing. "I'm waiting on Daysha," I say.

"Let's meet her at the airport or go to another hotel," Nevayah says.

"Why?" Yana asks.

"We been here too long," Nevayah says. "They gone find us. Shit. I'll be back." Soon as the door shuts Yana calls Daysha. She doesn't answer.

**Yana:** She stepped out. Hurry up and call.


"Where you at?" I ask.

"Gas station," Daysha says.

"Try to beat her back so we can go," I say.

"Grab my stuff," Daysha says.

I'm in the parking garage waiting on Yana to get back from seeing where Daysha's at.

Fuck. A car is coming. I get our shit and take the steps to the second floor. I see a shadow. "It's me," Daysha says.

Yana gets off the elevator and we leave.

"We switch flights and leave tomorrow," Daysha says. "We done with her ass."

"So where we going?" I ask.

"Somewhere close to the airport," Daysha says.


Me and Yana hear a glass break. Daysha dropped her water. "I fucked up our lives," she says. I kneel down next to her.

"We gone get out of here and start fresh," I say. Yana cleans up the glass.

"We supposed to be at your apartment cooking, drinking and smoking," Daysha says.

"Relax," Yana says.

"God not gone forgive us for this," Daysha says.

Aunt Genessa calls and asks where I'm at.

"I didn't make it," I say. "Can you get me, Yana and Daysha another flight?"

16

"Give me the phone," Aunt Genessa says.

"What are you doing?" I ask.

"Telling them to meet you at the airport," she says.

"I don't want to leave them," I say.

"Forget about them," Aunt Genessa says. "Traveling in packs when you're wanted is stupid. They don't need to know where you're at, your new name. None of that shit."

"I need to go back to the hotel and get the rest of my money," I say.

"No you don't," she says. "You need to get where lakes divide."

I text Daysha:

**Leilani:** Headed to the airport. Get another flight.

Aunt Genessa gives me Malcolm's number and address. He's who I'm staying with.

Me and Diego head to the airport. A car is hitting us from the back.

Diego turns on a siren and cars get out our way.

"You a cop?" I ask. He says no. "Why are we passing the airport exit?" I ask.

"Come two, come many," Diego says. "Don't get comfortable."

"Fuck!" I yell. Another car's hitting us. "Shit!"

When the light turns red, Diego speeds in front of the car that has green. Cops follow us. Diego speeds in front of the car entering the freeway, it slams on the brakes and is blocking the entrance. "We can make that exchange you wanted," he says to someone on the phone.

"I need to get to the airport," I say.

"Dead or alive?" Diego asks.

Diego parks on the curb in some neighborhood. He swaps keys with someone and we get in another car.

We're in airport traffic.

"A few years ago a couple cops tried to set my dad up for murder," Diego says. "They killed the wrong person, so they shot my dad and tried to plant a gun on him. I wasn't strapped so I called my cousins and they started shooting. They were gone clean up they mess, so while I rode with my dad to the hospital, my cousins cleaned up ours."

17

Me and Diego are still in airport traffic.

Fuck. Yana's being questioned by a security guard.

I'm looking for Daysha.

"Shit," I say. "Nevayah." She's standing in line at the outside check in. She's looking around. She stops when she sees Yana and gets out of line.

Daysha has her head in a brochure walking towards Yana.

I unlock my door and Diego locks it back. "It ain't shit you can do," he says.

Someone bumps into Daysha and she drops the brochure. She sees Yana talking to the security guard.

Diego puts his blinker on.

"What are you doing?" I ask.

"Even if you want to go to prison, I don't," Diego says.

The traffic's not moving.

Shit. Yana's security sees Daysha and she runs. He chases her and now Nevayah is running, and another security guard is running after her.

I get out the car and light a match I got from the hotel in a bag.

I toss the bag in the trash next to where Yana is. I pay a kid to pull the fire alarm. Yana's supervision leaves and so do we.

"Go!" I say to Diego.

"Look Lani," Yana says.

Daysha's being escorted into the back of a police car.

She sees us and looks down.

Diego puts his phone on speaker. "Junior, I need you to drive by my house," he says. "There's a key under the rug."

"Don't need it," Junior says. "It's unlocked. Your shit is fucked up. It's a few cars parked down the street. You know don't nobody just sit in the car around here not smoking shit."

Diego takes us to his cousins Eddie and Alexander's house.

"My man get rid of this fucking car," Eddie says.

Alexander says, "Locas," to me and Yana.

We walk in the house and The LA Four are on national news.

The airport scene is on replay.

The news reporter, Katie, is standing by the trash I lit on fire.

*"Daysha Vine was arrested today at the airport. As you can see here, Vine is running from security. Vine is a member of the LA Four. Police believe these women are all connected to the mass murder at the bank on third and the murder of Kenny Dane who was last seen entering into Vine's house."*

They're streaming pictures from me, Yana, Nevayah, and Daysha's social media accounts.

Katie is still talking.

*"They are running with Diego Martinez. The girls are here under fake passports. Vine isn't giving authorities any information on her friends."*

Diego and his friends are drinking beer.

"Ugly bitch," Yana says when she sees Trinity in an interrogation room.

Katie is still talking.

*"Here is the interview with Trinity Williams."*

"What made you decide to reveal everything you knew?" Mr. Carson asks.

"My conscience," Trinity says.

"You sure it didn't have anything to do with you almost dying in that explosion?" Mr. Carson asks. "Something tells me that wasn't part of the deal."

"I was supposed to put the bag in the bathroom and get the family there. No one was supposed to get hurt," Trinity says.

"What do you know about Kenny Dane?" Mr. Carson asks.

"We were friends a few years back," Trinity says.

"What happened?" Mr. Carson asks.

"He started mistreating Daysha so I left him alone," Trinity says.

"If I'm her," Alexander says. "I'd fuck ya'll up."

"A fuckin' Nightmare in Los Angeles," Eddie says.

Trinity's interview is still going.

"Look. I didn't know they were using real bombs," Trinity says.

"How did a bomb blow up the entire building without inside help?" Mr. Carson asks.

"Maybe someone else helped," Trinity says.

"Either she's a good liar, or Nevayah really had another connection," Alexander says. Him and Eddie look at each

60

other and say, "A good liar."

Trinity's interview is still going.

"Do you have another name you want to give us?" Mr. Carson asks.

"I don't know anything else," Trinity says.

"Did you know they were leaving town?" Mr. Carson asks.

"No," Trinity says.

Eddie turns the TV off.

"Look man, you can lay your head here for a while," Alexander says. "I can get you a boat."

"New identities…" Eddie says.

"They need new everything unless they want to be in the attic all day," Alexander says.

"Your faces gone be on poles," Eddie says.

"That shit gone be in people's windshield wipers," Alexander says.

"Basically what we're trying to say is, welcome to the club," Eddie says.

"He's the joker," Diego says.

Eddie turns the TV back on.

Daysha's being escorted back to the states.

Katie's talking.

*"U.S. officials promise to bring her to justice."*

Eddie turns the TV off.

Eddie shows me and Yana where the basement is. "If the cops come here, I'll kill them for you," Eddie says.

Yana lays down and I go back upstairs. Alexander is cooking. Eddie and Diego are drinking.

"Come on in," Eddie says to me.

"I already told her what happened with my dad," Diego says.

"Sorry about that," Eddie says to me.

"I'm sick of shit getting solved with death," Diego says.

"Things get solved with death sometimes," Eddie says and takes a shot. "You did what you needed to so you weren't the one attending a funeral."

Eddie sparks his blunt and gives it to me. "Is the drink gone do it for you?" he asks Diego. Diego says no. "I'll get you another one."

"Where's the bathroom?" I ask.

"In the hall on the right," Eddie says. The bathroom is the only room I've seen that's decorated with one color: red.

After I wash my hands I open the medicine cabinet and pills fall in the sink. I hear someone coming.

I open the door.

It's Eddie.

"It's amazing how fast someone will straighten up when their life is threatened," Eddie says.

"He's like this all the time," Alexander says.

"You will live, you will die, or you will be tortured forever," Eddie says.

"But he does know the truth," Alexander says. "No such thing as souls."

"Nothing can be undone," Eddie says.

"Enough with that scary shit Eddie," Diego says.

18

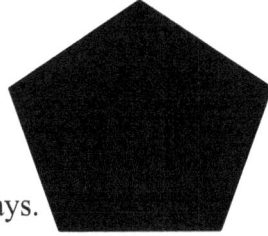

Yana's not in the basement.

"Check the bathroom," Eddie says.

The doors locked.

Alexander and Diego throw their bodies at the door and get it opened.

Yana's on the floor with a knife and bloody pill containers.

Diego and Eddie put her on the couch. "Call the ambulance and this is how you'll end up," Eddie says.

"Helen's on her way," Alexander says.

"She's a nurse," Diego says.

"One thing you need to know about the people that live in this house is we know some of everybody," Eddie says.

Yana's alright.

"Thanks for turning our living room into an ER," Eddie says to Helen then helps me clean up Yana's blood in the bathroom. "How did you meet Nevayah Harris?" he asks.

"School," I say.

"School taught me evil looks just like us," Eddie says. "There's a man named Jahod. His murder count never stops. I'm his son."

"Should I be scared of you?" I ask. He says yes. "Where's the trash?"

"I got it," Eddie says.

I sit next to Yana.

"I'd rather kill myself than let people torture me," Yana says.

"We're good," I say. "Eddie is crazy."

Eddie leaves and when he comes back says we're good to go.

"Everyone said yes?" Diego asks.

"You need me to get a tape recorder?" Eddie asks. "What about a glove?"

"He never quits," I say to Alexander.

"Never," Eddie says. "If you want a uniform, I can always make you one with green and red stripes."

"Thanks for your help," I say.

"The worst thing a murderer can do is lose a game of hide and seek," Eddie says.

"You got to have your own people," Alexander says. "Everybody on up to the damn president is fucked up."

"It's the people you never see that's responsible for murderers like my dad and me," Eddie says.

19

We're watching TV.

A reporter named Doris is talking.

*"Vine said she had no idea Harris was a killer. She admits to her part in being the getaway driver, but says all the lives taken were Harris' doing."*

"They lying about what they saying she said," Eddie says.

"Why won't they show her?" Yana asks.

"They not gone kill her until they find ya'll," Eddie says.

Doris is still talking.

*"If Vine can help bring in Nevayah Harris she could look at less time."*

"It don't matter if they find ya'll dead or alive," Eddie says. "You ever heard of anybody getting eighty years and walking out of prison? If you get that much time you were dead when you walked in."

The electricity cuts off.

It's pitch black. Alexander gets some flashlights.

Eddie uses a lighter.

"This happens every time it rains," Alexander says.

"I want to help Daysha get less time," I say.

"They lying about the deal," Eddie says.

"I still want to turn that bitch in," I say.

"Let's find that bitch," Yana says.

"And we can start with her damn weed supplier," I say.

"Check the lights," Eddie says.

The electricity's back on. Diego turns on the TV.

Mr. and Mrs. Vine are sitting in a courtroom behind Daysha and her lawyer.

"I thought her parents didn't like her," Yana says.

"They don't," I say.

"Lawyers set they own people up," Eddie says and takes a gun out the closet.

Lightening hits and glass drops in the kitchen.

Eddie cleans it up.

Yana pulls me to the side. "If," Yana says. "We put all the deaths on Nevayah. We didn't know shit about Kenny. We left and came back. She was still by herself."

"Ya'll not getting caught," Eddie says. "Aye you still talk to that fool in L.A. that you went to prison for?" he asks Alexander.

"Deon," Alexander says. "Hell yea."

"Make the call," Eddie says.

20

Deon's at my Grandma Cedes house as a pizza man.

He's not posing.

That's where he works.

Grandma Cedes went and saw Daysha and Deon's going to deliver us the message.

"She wants you guys to find Nevayah," Deon says.

"And what else?" Eddie asks.

"That's it," Deon says. "Just find her. What you got me into man? You know I can't get another strike."

"I can do worse than another strike," Eddie says.

"She said somebody pushed her at the airport," Deon says. "She thinks Nevayah told him to do it because when she was being handcuffed she saw her. She didn't want to take a chance on the other two girls getting caught, so she didn't say nothing."

"What about the aunt?" Eddie asks.

"I told her ya'll gone find Nevayah," Deon says. "She told me Daysha's parents are trying to get all they asses locked up. She said don't trust her."

"Get on a flight out here," Eddie says.

"What?" Deon yells.

"Nigga lower your mutha fuckin' voice," Eddie says.

"You know I can't go back to Mexico," Deon says.

"I didn't ask you a question," Eddie says. "Make sure you got more than one pizza uniform."

Eddie hangs up. "The weed supplier," he says looking at me.

"He lived somewhere close to the hotel we were at," I say. "Nevayah would leave and get back quick. She can't go long without smoking that shit. I know she taking in more than she ever has now. She gone have somebody getting that shit for her."

"If she could get her weed fast, the spot wasn't far," Diego says.

"Pack some clothes," Eddie says.

Me and Yana go downstairs.

When we get back upstairs the house is empty.

The boys are in a van.

We get in.

Eddie's on the phone.

Jahod's giving him spots to swing by.

21

Eddie takes me, Yana, Alexander and Diego to a room.

Deon calls and says he's on his way.

Eddie's talking to a dealer on the corner. He gets back in the car and me and Diego get out. We follow the dealer and he goes to a house party.

We sit on a bench close by while Eddie, Deon, Alexander and Yana are watching other dealers.

The boy we're stalking comes out the party with friends. They go to an alley and smoke.

"I hope they get them bitches," one of the boys says.

"They got Mexico fucked up," one of the girls says.

The L.A. Four are the talk of the country.

"If I see them bitches I'm shooting them straight in they heart," another girl says.

Me and Diego meet the crew at a fast food place. They're done eating when we walk in.

"There's thousands," Eddie says. "Tomorrow."

On the drive back to the hotel Eddie recognizes someone. "That's my boy Esko," he says and pulls over. "We gone find that bitch tonight. If she a weed-head like you say, he done seen her or know somebody that know her."

Eddie says something and Esko shakes his head no.

He's lying.

Eddie's walking backwards to the car with his hand in his pocket ready to take out his gun.

A man runs up and shoots Eddie.

It's Nathan.

Nevayah's brother.

Eddie's falling and shooting, people are running and screaming and Diego's getting in the driver's seat.

Alexander tries to get out the car and Diego locks the door.

"He's gone," Diego says.

The sirens get louder.

"Get the fuck out of here man!" Deon yells.

"Shut the fuck up," Diego says and speeds off.

I still see Nathan get in a car with Esko and Nevayah.

When we get to the hotel, Deon gets in a cab and leaves. Alexander gets in the driver's seat and leaves.

Me and Yana are getting our stuff together.

"Eddie's dead," Diego says. He's drinking out the bottle. He punches me in the face. I fall to the floor. Yana hits him in the head with the lamp.

He's unconscious.

Me and Yana use lamp cords to tie Diego's arms and legs together.

I find a gun in the dresser.

The first thing Diego sees is the gun at his head. "Tell Deon to get us a car," I say.

22

"Money first," Deon says.

Me and Yana are good to go.

We're circling the block I saw Nevayah on.

Kids are standing on the corner. They run slow enough so we can see which house they go in.

We're about to make that bitch come out.

Esko is walking down the street.

I pull over next to some kids playing kickball. "Who wants to make a hundred dollars?" I ask.

"Doing what?" one of the boys asks.

I give the kid the matches, gas and a bottle. "Throw it through 316," I say. I give him the money. "I can give you guys the same amount if you do the same thing," I say to his friends."

They all say okay.

The kids throw the lit bottles, paper and shirts, and sticks through different windows in the house and run like hell.

The house goes up in flames. Nevayah runs out.

"Fuck!" I scream.

"Shit!" Yana screams.

The bad ass kids are knocking on my window.

"Anytime," one says.

"Nice gun," another one says.
Fire trucks, ambulances and police cars are here.
I get on the interstate and go to a rest stop.
I answer Diego's phone.
"I'll find you."
It's Jahod.

Me and Yana go to a motel.

The administrator has on raggedy clothes and looks bitter. He's the person I was hoping would be here. I put money on the counter. He counts it, looks at me, then Yana. Then at a poster with our faces on it.

I put another hundred on the counter. He rips the poster and gives me a key.

Deon texts Diego's phone telling him to have me call him.

"What do you want?" I ask.

"I want you to help me and I can help you," Deon says. "You have Diego's phone and it has Jahod's number. Every person that smokes weed is looking for you and there's a price on your head. You need help."

"I'm listening," I say.

"I can call Jahod and say Alexander and Diego set his son up," Deon says.

"What do you want?" I ask.

"Tomorrow they're taking Daysha to Densick Prison," Deon says. "That's where my sister is locked up. Daysha is getting life and she's serving it with Trinity and soon Nevayah. Give me something to say that will get her to escape with my sister. You're not going to make it another day out here with Jahod after you."

Someone's walking up and down the hall ringing a bell.

The alarm says 8:16AM. "The fuck is going on?" I ask.

Yana's looking out the peephole. "Shhhh," she says to me. "Listen."

"Get over here!" a woman yells. The bell stops.

"I don't think anyone's here mommy," a kid says.

What the fuck does he mean he doesn't think anyone's here?

Cars are pulling in the parking lot.

Me and Yana lean the beds against the door.

Deon doesn't answer.

Gunshots!

"We better off in here," I say. "I know someone's watching this window."

The gunshots stop. The beds are moving.

Diego's phone rings.

"Open the door," Deon says. I open the door and he says, "Follow him. His name is Eden"

We pass a lot of dead bodies. Two are Diego and Alexander's.

Eden opens the front door and someone shoots at us.

We stay in until Deon says, "Come on."

We're on the interstate.

The glass in the car behind us shatters.

Yana gets shot.

A car flips over. That car hits another car and the

explosion blocks everyone trying to kill us.

A woman named Maria pulls the bullet out and stitches Yana up.

"Your friend helps my daughter get out of prison," Maria says. Now she's taking a bullet out of one of her crew members. When she finishes, Eden, the man from the motel, and her other security guard Wilson go outside and smoke a blunt and Maria takes me and Yana to the guest room. "Jahod never stops. They're in L.A. waiting for you. If you see a police car, they'll be the ones driving." She takes a picture of Yana's wound for Deon to show Daysha.

"Jahod has a lot of people that will kill for him," Maria says. "But not as many as me. Before he became the man he is, he worked for me. We never had bad blood until today when I killed his men to save you two. You will help me."

Me and Yana follow her to another room. "Her names Abigail," Maria says holding a picture. "I sent her to L.A. to see her dad. The bastard got drunk and raped her. When he went to sleep Abby stabbed him in his neck. She got his ass three times. When Abby walked out, her dad's girlfriend walked up. Abby fought her. The neighbors called the police."

Maria brings me and Yana some liquor, weed and food.

"It's all coming back to you, huh?" Yana asks.

"Hell yea," I say.

"The games and parties," Yana says.

"Abby just found out there's a new driver for those kids that visit the prison," Maria says. "She's not sure about the officer anymore now that her partner is your friend. You two are going back to L.A."

Maria's friend's Pedro and Rick are going to take me and Yana to meet the driver of the truck at a rest stop. "There's an extra wall that doesn't look like it's there," Maria says. "That's what Abigail and Daysha will hide behind. The wall is easy to slide over and back. Abigail knows people that work in the kitchen. I'll be sending them money."

Maria gives me and Yana masks that look like real people, Perry's Produce badges with our new faces already on them and phones.

In L.A. we get in a car with Peter, Maria's brother.

We pull into a gated house. Ariana, Maria's sister, is waiting by the door. She's picking us up from the rest stop after we get the girls.

The plan is the girls get out, we meet at the stop, drive to the shore and Peter sails us off.

Me and Yana get to the rest stop and get in the truck.

The keys are already in the ignition.

The guards check my Perry's Produce badge.

"Never seen you before," one says.

"Good," I say. "And how are you today?"

"I work at a prison," he says.

I drive through the grass and get close to the back door of the kitchen.

Two guards are drinking coffee.

By the back door.

I leave the truck running.

Yana gives me the crate with the money.

An old prisoner gets a crate and we follow her. Another prisoner gets the crate that has the bombs in them. We sit the crates on a counter. When me and the old prisoner get outside she falls to the ground. "Can I get some help?!" the old prisoner yells at the guards.

The guards grab a few crates. "Over here!" the old lady yells. They go to the side of the building.

The bombs go off.

Yana, Daysha and Abigail get in the truck.

I pull the fuck off.

Police cars are at the rest stop. They're talking to Ariana and the man who owns the Perry's Produce truck I'm in.

I drive past the stop.

Cops are following us.

I call Maria.

"Have Abby get the red crate," Maria says.

Yana, Daysha and Abigail slide the back door up, dump gas on the road and light it.

Fire everywhere.

Abigail's shooting gas on the cars.

No one is around us anymore.

Maria's calling back. "Get rid of the truck," she says.

I go to an empty parking lot in a warehouse area.

I let the girls out the back. Abigail's squirting gasoline all over the truck.

She gives Maria the cross streets then gets another crate out the truck. She gives us all a gun and uses a remote to blow the truck up.

Cars are pulling up. They're not honking.

We run to the warehouse. All the doors are locked.

We throw bricks through the window.

# 29

I'm hiding behind boxes in a room. Our guest greet us with a gun shot in the air.

"Come out bitch," someone says and shoots again. I hear people walking every direction. "Fuck Mexico. I'll kill your ass here." Someone shoots at my door. I go in the room next to me. "My name's Kenneth Dane. I'm Kenny's brother." Someone shoots and I hear shit falling upstairs. Kenneth's voice is getting closer to me. I'm ducked down behind the boxes. Gun ready to shoot. "The nerve of you, you fuckin' bitch, to try and deny us a burial for my brother," Kenneth says.

Now there's a series of gunshots.

Someone shoots the lock off my door. "Daysha!" It's Kenneth screaming.

He's kicking and pushing shit. Coming right towards me, still shooting.

I shoot his leg and run, then duck. Someone else is shooting at me. I run in another room. It's a stairway. I hop over the man lying dead in it.

When I open the door to the second floor a gun is pointed at me.

It's Abigail.

She lowers it.

We go downstairs and hear someone open the door.

We run upstairs to a room, lock the door and shoot the windows.

Kenneth shoots the lock off the door.

"Where the fuck is Daysha?" Kenneth yells.

Daysha walks up behind him and shoots him in the back of his head. "Right here," Daysha says.

We hear another gunshot and someone fall over the railing. We all have our guns pointed at the door.

It's Eden.

We pull into a boarding dock. Peter's here.

I see two cops. "Leilani, meet my cousins Andrew and Silky," Eden says.

Me, Yana, Daysha and Abigail follow Peter on the boat. Someone's pouring a drink at the mini bar.

"Help yourselves," Ariana says.

Peter makes sure we're all here and we leave.

"The fire had them cops asking questions," Ariana says.

"Whose boat is this?" I ask.

"Mine," Maria says coming downstairs.

I'm the first one to wake up when we stop. I go upstairs.

"Welcome to Panama," Peter says.

"Where's Abigail and Maria?" I ask.

"Back in Mexico," Peter says.

"There's a car parked around front," Peter says giving me the keys.

Yana and Daysha come upstairs.

"We never mention it," I say.

www.ingramcontent.com/pod-product-compliance
Lightning Source LLC
Chambersburg PA
CBHW050557280326
41933CB00011B/1884